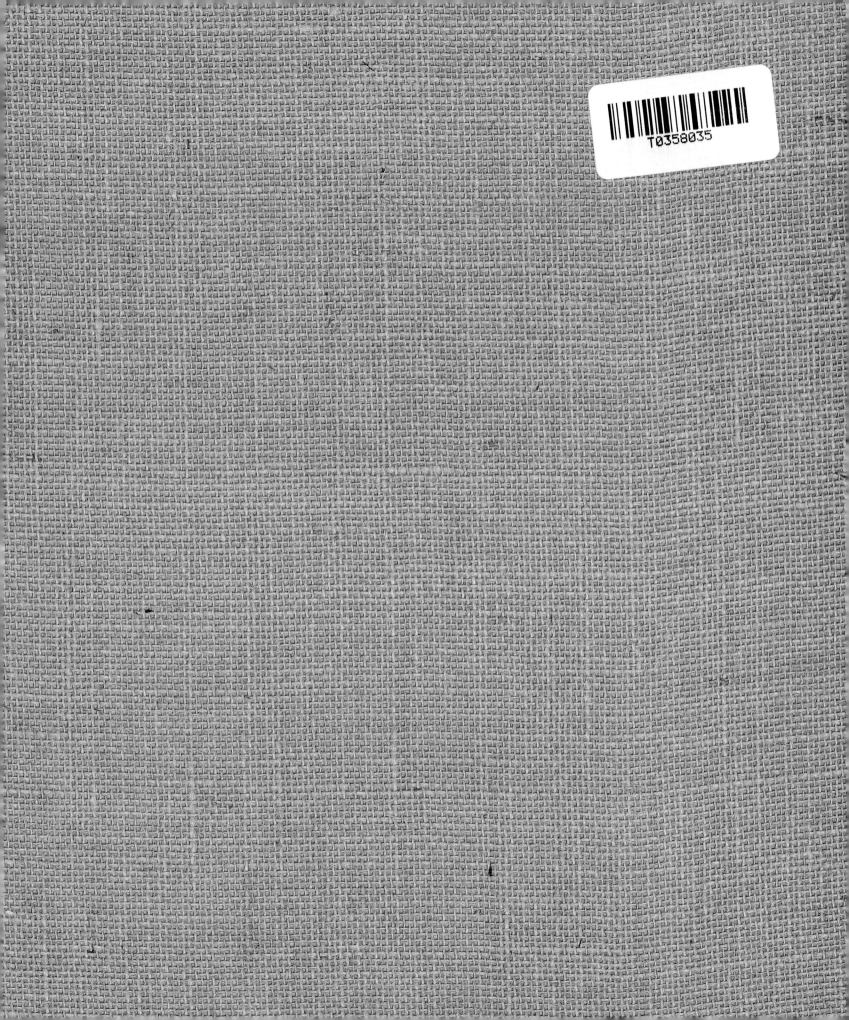

GUFF

AARON BLABEY

PENGUIN|VIKING

For the Permanents and the Rotations . . .

VIKING

UK | USA | Canada | Ireland | Australia | India | New Zealand | South Africa | China

Penguin Books is part of the Penguin Random House group of companies whose
addresses can be found at global.penguinrandomhouse.com.

Penguin
Random House
Australia

First published by Penguin Random House Australia Pty Ltd, 2017

3 5 7 9 10 8 6 4 2

Cover and text design by Aaron Blabey and Marina Messiha
Colour separation by Splitting Image Colour Studio, Clayton, Victoria
Printed and bound in China.

National Library of Australia Cataloguing-in-Publication data:
Blabey, Aaron, author, illustrator
Guff/ Aaron Blabey (author/illustrator)

ISBN: 978 0 67 007717 5 (hbk.)
For pre-school age.
Children's stories.

penguin.com.au

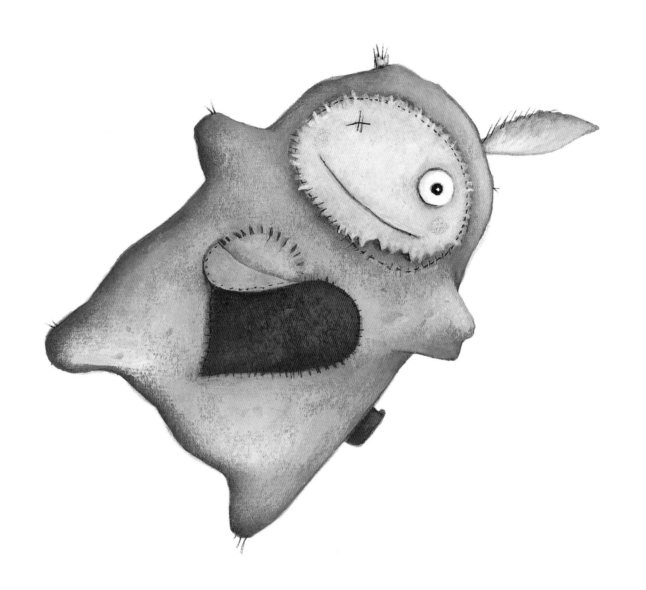

This is my Guff.

He's really nice.

I've known him since I was little.

And I still know him
even now I'm big.

He's just great.

Well, mostly he is.

But even when he's naughty . . .

I still really love him.

Because I always know he's there.

Well, almost always.

Sometimes he goes missing.

I worry about him.

But then he always turns up.

Silly old Guff.

I know sometimes he's a bit stinky.

And sometimes, he's even a bit boring.

But I don't care about any of that.

Because he's my Guff.